# ZERO ADVERTISING COST BLOG COMMENTING ROCKS

An Undiscovered Traffic Source for Any Business

# Harshajyoti Das

# Dedication

To my wife

# About the Author

## Harshajyoti Das

Harsh is the CEO and Co-Founder of Munmi IT Solutions LLP.

He is a traveler, a writer, an inbound marketer, an entrepreneur, and a business adviser.

His other books, "How to write content that converts 600% More" and "No SEO Forever" are both bestsellers. He has published over 7 books and is writing his 8th book.

He is also the founder of FireYourMentor.com, a platform for self-published authors.

# LET'S CONNECT !

*I offer all my new releases for either FREE or at $0.99 to all my readers during the launch day. To get notified about the launch, sign up to my mailing list.*

### *Do sign up as a fan here:*

http://www.fireyourmentor.com/70-secrets-revealed/

*(I hate spam as much as you do).*

## Contact Info:

- **Fan Email:** author@harsh.im
- **Interview/guestposting/Press requests:** press@harsh.im
- **Amazon Author Profile:** http://www.amazon.com/author/harshajyotidas
- **Twitter:** http://twitter.com/jr_sci
- **Facebook:** https://www.facebook.com/harshajyotidas.author
- **LinkedIn:** http://in.linkedin.com/pub/harshajyoti-das/17/28b/52
- **Google+:**

https://plus.google.com/+HarshajyotiDas

**Author Website:** Harsh.Im

**CEO at Munmi IT Solutions LLP:** Munmi.org

**Founder of:** FireYourMentor.com

# Table of Contents

The Changing Online Marketing World

Five Principles of Persuasion

It's Not Just a Feedback Form

Advantages of Blog Commenting

How to Use Blog Commenting More Effectively?

My Personal Tips for You

Do's and Don'ts

A Note to My Readers

Review If You Want, I Won't Force You

# The Changing Online Marketing World

MySpace, Orkut and Friendster were doing great in 2004. Once Facebook and Twitter came into the picture, they were wiped off the face of the earth.

The online marketing world has been changing quite rapidly in the last decade. Twitter and Facebook are doing great now, but will they be around in ten years? I don't know. Do you?

Is it really worth investing hundreds or thousands of dollars on advertising to gain likes and followers? Maybe it is, but only if you can get a positive ROI within a year, but a long-term plan doesn't work quite as well.

Moreover, you have no absolute control over these big companies. Organic engagement and reach are decreasing on social media day by day. Any small policy change will affect your whole business strategy.

You need to look out for alternatives while there is still time. Exploit all the traffic channels available to you. Do not just rely on Google, Facebook and Twitter for traffic.

In this book, I will talk about one such traffic source. BLOGS!

Blogs came into the picture in the late 1990's. Blogspot.com was launched in 1999 and then Wordpress in 2011. Since then, both of them have grown exponentially.

Blogs have been here a long time and are still doing pretty well. They have held their position in the market when everything else was changing around us.

There's fierce competition when you talk about the online marketing world. Half a billion advertising agencies are moving online. Don't you think the competition is going to get even higher?

Whether it's SEO, Adwords, Facebook, Twitter, PPC, PPV, banner advertising or Email marketing, competition is at an all-time high.

It has become immensely important that we look for alternative traffic sources. The answer is "Blog Commenting." It's still an undiscovered reserve of traffic. Thus, the idea to write this book was born.

# Chapter 1

## Five Principles of Persuasion

If you haven't read *Influence* by Robert Cialdini, you have missed out on a very good book regarding marketing. In this chapter, I will talk about the five principles of persuasion and how you can use them with blog commenting.

**What does blog commenting have in common with the six persuasion techniques by Robert Cialdini?**

Let's revise the five principles of persuasion. They are reciprocity, social proof, likeability, authority and commitment.

### Reciprocity

There are numerous instances where reciprocity manipulates us into going on almost an auto-pilot mode. Think of it from a real life experience. When somebody gives you an expansive watch on your birthday, don't you feel like giving them something expensive on their birthday as well?

In the online world, the effect of reciprocity is even higher. When somebody likes you on Facebook, you start liking their posts as well. I can see that you are starting to think about it. Good. Think about more such instances. When somebody calls you for dinner, you feel obliged to call them for dinner as well.

Human psychology can be manipulated and smart marketers have been manipulating us for a very long time. Let's see how we can use the power of reciprocity to our advantage using blog commenting.

**Try out this exercise:**

Go to any blog and compliment an article. Write a good comment as to why you like it and offer some of your own input to add more value to that article. Make sure that the comment is at least 300 words long. You want to make an impact. Wait two to three days for the comment to get approved. Once done, follow the guy on Twitter and ask him to tweet one of your articles. You will be surprised to see that almost all of them will comply with your request. No matter how busy they are or how big they are, they will be happy to return the favor. Sounds impossible, right? Try it.

With blog commenting, your primary idea

should be to build a relationship with a blogger with a huge audience. To build a relationship, you need to genuinely care about that person. If you keep your selfish interests at heart, it will reveal itself.

Start by tweeting, liking and commenting on every post he/she publishes. With each action, you are contributing value to the blogger. It's similar to exchanging gifts in the real world.

Tell me one thing. When you buy a gift for someone, do you ask anything in return? Of course not. Still, the other person ends up buying you a gift anyway. Think about this. What would have happened if you would have asked the other person for a return gift to his/her face? It would be awkward. The same thing happens when you ask for a favor immediately after offering value to a blogger. We need to have patience to receive our reward, instead of asking for it.

While commenting on blogs, build a relationship with the blogger and wait for your rewards. Don't ask the blogger for favors. It shows your shallowness instantly.

With time, the blogger will recognize you as an active member of the community or a supporting friend. Once, you are in the limelight, the blogger will befriend you and will help you succeed.

**This actually opens you up to a lot of opportunities. Let me list a few:**

1. No waiting time for your comment to get approved
2. Links inside comment becomes acceptable
3. Guest posting/interview opportunities
4. Banner advertising priority
5. Mentions on blog and social networks
6. A new friend with a huge audience

It's always easier to succeed when you have many helping hands instead of just two. As you hop from one blog to the other, you will make a lot of friends in the process. You are not promoting yourself by commenting on these blogs. You are making friends with the blog owner and his audience.

Tomorrow, there can be a guy from the audience who might invite you to do an interview or might want to form a JV to sell your products. You never know what opportunities are likely to open.

**Social proof**

When you are everywhere, people will start knowing you by your contribution as a blog commenter. If you write valuable comments, they will trust what you say. You will make friends with authority figures. Apart from all these advantages, you will also build social proof, and I will tell you how.

It's obvious you will build a following whenever you have a new product or a service. Let's say you have launched a new Ebook on your site.

Whenever you launch a product or a service, you can just send a message to your friends and followers and they will jump to promote you.

**If you can make friends with an influencer, imagine what a single tweet might do to your overall launch strategy. His one testimonial can be enough to motivate thousands of others to buy your product. You will have no shortage of testimonials or reviews with all these influencers backing you up as one of their own.**

When your tribe consists of people who really care about you, it becomes really easy to promote any product or a service with their help. You don't even have to ask for their help. They will come forward and offer you their help. That's the power of building relationships.

When you start your commenting spree, it will

eventually increase your social following on Twitter, Facebook and on LinkedIn. It will offer you social proof.

It's only obvious that a person with 50,000 Twitter followers is more likely to impress a new customer than a person with 300 Twitter followers. Got the idea?

**LIKEABILITY**

People will start linking you when you continuously add value to their article. In the online world, we get excited when we get a like from someone on Facebook. We get even more excited when we get a comment on a funny picture that we posted a couple of hours back.

A comment on your blog will make you even more excited than a like on Facebook. The reason being, your blog is like your baby. It's a part of you. When someone praises an article you wrote, they are actually praising you. And who doesn't like that?

When a commenter repeatedly comments on your blog every time you post an article, of course you will start liking him.

Likeability is a very powerful tool for influence. It puts a person in the auto-pilot mode. When a person I like recommends a book to me, I immediately buy it. If they ask me for a favor, such as a request to provide feedback on their new website design or to write a testimonial for their new product, I always oblige. The reason being, I feel an ethical obligation towards that person. You can't say it's always an obligation. It just makes me happy when I help a person I like.

There was a study conducted where a car salesman sold hundreds of cars in a month. It turned out that he had a very simple sales tactic. He makes his clients LIKE him. Every month, he sends out a letter to all his clients with a simple message, "I like you."

As a marketer you will need all the "professional" friends you can have. You need to form allies with a lot of people to promote each other's products. Each one of your can leverage the "likeability" factor to sell to your audience.

Let's say you and I both have a similar product. We have our respective audiences, who love and adore us. If you promote your product to my audience, they might not buy it. They will be skeptical. Most of them will just turn you off and delete your cold email. But what if I introduce you to them? What if I recommend your product to my audience? They already like me. They will trust me when I recommend your product. That's the difference between cold-calling and product recommendation from a person whom they "like."

In order to form this alliance, you need to build a connection with all of the influencers in your industry. You can surely connect to them on social networks, but most of all you can connect with them on their personal blogs via blog commenting.

Blog commenting is the base of the funnel. You can start with blog commenting to build a connection and then end up owning an audience of hundreds of thousands of people who love and adore you. Blog commenting is the key to the door that will open millions of opportunities.

**AUTHORITY:**

When someone Googles your name, he will come across all these comments you have posted.

It builds your authority and online reputation. You come out as someone who is knowledgeable in his/her industry.

When you have a brand, it helps your brand to battle negative press. When someone searches for your brand name, your comments will show up instead of negative press. Google loves fresh content, hence a comment on a newly published article (in your industry) has a better chance of showing up on the front page of Google.

Apart from online reputation management, blog commenting helps you portray yourself as a highly skilled personal. Your knowledge will be evident based on the quality of blog comments you write.

Commenting on a blog owned by an influencer makes more sense. When you add additional value to an article with your blog comment, you will come out as someone who has the same authority as the influencer. It puts you in the league of highly influential people.

If the blog owner is immensely happy with your commenting skills, you might get an invitation to write a guest post on his blog. Imagine the authority you will build when you open all these opportunities.

With every comment you make, it shows your authority on a subject. Hence, it's important that you leave a comment with value instead of a one-liner that says, "Thank you for writing this article."

### CONSISTENCY and COMMITMENT:

Consistency is the key. When your name pops up repeatedly on a site, everyone will wonder, "Who is this guy?"

Commit yourself to comment on at least five to ten blogs daily.

You need to be consistent with your commitment to comment. Let a content owner feel that you will come back and enhance the value of their content. The consistency in blog commenting will open opportunities to guest post on many prominent blogs. Whenever they publish a blog post, they will be waiting for you to come and post a comment on their blog. Put yourself in the shoes of a blog owner. Wouldn't you want to see more commenting on your blog?

It takes time for everything to form a habit, especially for tasks such as blog commenting that takes time and effort. You will need to read the entire article before posting your comment. The comment is again around 200 to 300 words. The whole process is new for us and it takes commitment from our end to include a new task in our busy schedule.

We need to make it a habit so that it comes naturally, without any effort. I used to struggle writing even 100 words. With time and practice, it takes me less than ten minutes to write 300 words.

Commitment is building your will power, while consistency to forms a habit. Will power will run out after a couple of days, but habit is forever.

# Chapter 2

# It's Not Just a Feedback Form

The comment field is often misunderstood as just a feedback form. There's so much possibility hiding behind the comment form.

If you go to any popular blog, you will find a lot of comments on each article. You need to stand out for the crowd or else no one will notice you. Worst case scenario, your effort will go to waste because you were lost in the crowd.

In this chapter we will talk about how we can write a comment that can stand out from the crowd.

### Be the first to comment in order to stay in the top position

This is perhaps the most important advice I can offer in this chapter. You want your comment to be visible. If a blog post has 50 comments and your comment is somewhere in the 33rd position, it won't get you any visibility.

Your goal should be to stay on top of all the comments that are being posted for that article. How do you stay on top? Well, the answer to this question is simple. You should be the first one to comment on that blog post.

Just two days back, my buddy Ryan published a 7000 word mega blog post on his blog. As soon as I saw his update on Facebook, I knew this blog post was going to be one of the most popular blog posts he has every written in his blog. I had to grab the opportunity to be the first one to comment. I was busy with other things, but I had to prioritize. I stopped what I was doing and started speed-reading his article. Within 15 minutes, I was done and had left a comment on his site. Since I have already built a connection with him, he has whitelisted my comments. My comments go live instantly on his site (no moderation queue). I was relieved when I saw that I was the first to comment on his post.

Here's the blog post:
http://www.bloggingfromparadise.com/ebook-10-4/

Within two days, he had already received 17 comments. I am sure he is going to hit at least 100 comments within a month's time.

Being on top of all the comments has given me a lot of visibility. Just think about it. If the same folks who have seen my name in this blog post happen to surf through Amazon and see one of my books, what are the chances that they will buy my book? It's definitely going to be 100% times more than someone who has never heard my name. That's personal branding.

So, can you always be the first one to post a comment?

There's no secret. Just be friends with the blog owner on Facebook, Twitter or LinkedIn. As soon as the blog post goes live, they will usually share it with their social network.
You can also sign up to their mailing list, but most authors will send it out to their list after one to two days. It still works if you are not able to make a connection with the blog owners directly.

**If not, reply to the first comment to stay in the second position**

Sometimes, you might not be the first one to post a comment. There might be someone who has already posted his/her comment.

In such cases you can use a simple trick: **Reply to the first comment**

There will always be something to say to the first commenter. What I do is to try to add value to the already posted comment. Try to relate to what the first commenter has said and draft your own comment.

The main idea behind blog commenting is not to gain a backlink or to drive traffic. Our goal is to brand ourselves, to increase our visibility in the online world. You need to think of it like old-school advertising.

Once you are clear on your goals, you will find more ways to increase your visibility. Let's say an article is immensely popular. You might want to reply to each and every person who has commented. That way, your visibility grows by 100% with each new reply.

**Treat it as an extension of the article**

Our comment is an extension of the original article. We have the opportunity to add value to the original article. Once we read a blog post, we often come up with a lot of queries. No matter how well-researched and descriptive an article is, we always feel that there's something that's being left out.

We can take those queries and make a list. We can write our own little article to solve these queries. Then, post that article in the comments field. It will be like a mini-guest post that will add more value to the original article.

You are not just creating a brand, but you are helping people by solving their queries. A comment field gives you instant access to post on any blog. Why not use it to write our own little article that will be posted below the original article?

Once we form a habit of writing comments that serve as an extension of the article, we will get recognized by the creator of the article. We might well get a chance to write a guest article on that blog. These small steps can open a wide range of opportunities in front of us.

**Treat it like a guest post**

We need to form a habit of writing comments that are like guest posts. There's no point in writing a one- or two-liner comment until it's absolutely necessary.

Earlier, we talked about writing an extension of the article. I want to clarify what I meant by writing an extension. Some people might think that an extension needn't be worth 300 words. A 50 word comment to point out a couple of queries will suffice. Wrong! Your comment should be like a mini-guest post. It's absolutely tough to get your hands on big blogs when it comes to guest articles. Most of the popular blogs will accept guest authors based on invitation only. When you have the alternate route to reach thousands of visitors with a blog comment alone, why not exploit this opportunity to the fullest?

**Make the content more valuable**

If we don't add value, people can see that. It's very easy to leave a quick comment for the sake of it, but it is of no good to you or the visitors. Your comment should have a core value. Whenever we post a comment on a blog, we should ask ourselves, "What value am I offering via my comment?" If we can't find a good enough answer to our question, it means that we should work hard to offer some superior value via our comments.

A reader will recognize when you offer valuable advice via your comments. The blog owner will also recognize your potential. Even the journalists who lurk around blogs to find a source for their story will also find you.

I am a spiritual guy (not religious though). I believe in karma. When you offer value, you build good karma for yourself. The universe will reward you by opening a window of opportunities in front of you. When you offer good karma, you receive good karma. It's so amazing to see how these rewards come easily to us once we start adding value.

A couple of months back, I was surfing through some articles on marketing in Huffington Post. I saw an interview of Matthew Capala from searchdecoder.com. A couple of days before he has published his book called, "SEO Like I'm 5." Since I was also a SEO'r in my previous life, I posted a comment where I put my opinion in front of the audience. I checked out his blog and posted a comment even there. Two days later, he added me on LinkedIn and Twitter and invited me for an interview on his blog.

My point is, when you add value, people can see that. Similarly, when you post a comment with absolutely no value, even then people can recognize it. What we give is what we get. We need to remember that.

**Add personal experiences**

There are thousands of articles on the web telling the exact same thing. Try reading an article on "how to sleep early." Any article you read will have 80% similarity with each other. They talk about going to bed early, exercising during the day, having food at least 2 hours before sleeping, having a light supper and meditation.

When the content you read talks about the same stuff, it cannot make an imprint on a reader's mind. Our brains need new information to remember. The same information bores the hell out of our brains. So, what's one thing that can make your content unique?

The answer is *your personal experience from your own life.*

Nobody on this planet has shared the exact fate you have. No one else has gone through the same circumstances that you have. Our personal experiences are what make our story unique. With every comment, try to put a story from your own life.

Adding a personal story to your comment will make it stand out of the crowd. Even the blog owner will be happy to interact and know you a little bit better.

**Add anecdotes stories to the content**

When you can't find any similarity with your own life, then what? There's of course a possibility that you will read an article that has absolutely no relevance with your life. How will you add a personal story then?

In those cases, think about other people you know. Your friends, family members, business associates, neighbors, friends of friends, Twitter followers or even a guy who sent you hate mail.

Try to see if you can tell a story about one of these people. We as human beings adore listening or reading stories. It's not a new trend. Stories have evolved from the caveman era. Our ancestors used to make up stories of how the sun was eaten by a demon in a solar eclipse 4500 years ago.

When you add anecdotes or a story to your comment, it stands out. Our goal is to become more visible and this strategy helps us fulfill it.

**Try to write a better article**

Can you write a piece of content better than the original creator of the blog post? If yes, do it. Show your authority on the subject. You might have decades of experience in a particular industry, whereas the blog owner might be just starting out.

Your comment should show superior excellence and your years of experience. Everybody can recognize an elephant in the room. Be one.

I always encourage people to start a business based on what they love doing. When the basic principle to build a business is right, it becomes even easier to build a brand. You can talk about your niche better than anybody else in the industry. When it comes to blog commenting, you can write a comment that will show that you have decades of experience in that niche. Make each and every blog comment count.

## Shift the focus from the main article to your blog commenter

Your comment should be so good that the attention should shift from the main article to your comment. Can you do that? Why don't you try an exercise today. Find any article in your niche. Then write a comment worth double the word count of that article. Post it. See what happens.

You will be adored, loved and respected by all the readers, including the blog owner. Your superiority and authority will come to the surface with absolutely no sales pitch. You just need to deliver your knowledge and people are smart enough to recognize talent.

But everything comes down to taking that first leap. So, stop reading this book for a while and go back and write a comment with double the word count. You will be amazed with the response you will get from other commenters. They will start replying to your comment instead of the original article.

When you can shift the focus from the main article to your comment, you can consider yourself a winner.

# Chapter 3

## Advantages of Blog Commenting

When there are hundreds of other advertising opportunities, why should we only focus on blog commenting? People who haven't heard the concept of blog commenting struggle to understand the "real" advantages of blog commenting.

In this chapter, we will talk about a couple of advantages of blog commenting. You are free to add a list of advantages if you can come up with some new ideas. Feel free to add more value when you will review this book on Amazon.

### It's free, unlike sponsored posts

Have you ever brought a sponsored post on a blog? If yes, then you will know how much it cost you for a single article. If you haven't brought a sponsored article yet, then let me tell you that it costs around $1000.00 for a single sponsored blog post on an average blog.

With blog commenting you are cutting out the

unnecessary fees. You can post a 1000 word long comment in any article for absolutely zero advertising cost. You will offer the same knowledge, you will reach the same audience, but there will be a big difference of the $1000.00.

So why aren't people already doing it already?

You will be amazed to hear this, but a lot of people have already been exploiting this gold mine. A selective few have discovered the secrets before any of us. It's better late than never. I have told you the secret, now it's time to take action.

Comments are free. If we receive something for free, we have the natural tendency to take things for granted. I will give you an example. Let's say you visit a blog with an Alexa rank of 1000. They charge $5000.00 for each sponsored post. For a limited time, they have discounted the price for one sponsored post to just $100.00. I bet each and everyone who is reading this book will jump on that offer.

When the same blog allows visitors to post comments completely free of charge, nobody gives a damn. Some people do take a minute or two and post a one-liner and then leave. Do you see how irrational human beings can be?

I know some of your will say that a comment doesn't receive the same visibility as a blog post. I completely agree. There's no denying that. But you will also agree with me when I say that a comment will receive at least 10% of the visibility of a normal article, if not the same?

What's 10% of a $5000.00 sponsored post? Each and every comment you post on that blog will be worth $500.00. The blog owner gives you a free pass to post a comment that would have usually cost you $500.00 to achieve the same visibility.

**No pending queue like guest posting. It gets accepted within a matter of hours**

I have tried guest posting and I can tell you one thing. It takes a massive amount of time and energy. First, you need to pitch your ideas to the blog owner. It takes weeks to receive a reply. In most cases, 99% will choose to ignore your request. The worst part is that some blog owners will ask for money to publish a guest article. What?

Even if you get accepted to write an article, you will have to go through a rigorous give and take to edit, add and remove content from your article to suit their audience. It again takes months for the article to go live.

After spending hours researching, writing and

then weeks waiting for the article to get published, the article might not send enough traffic. There are a lot of business owners who have reported that the time spent in publishing these guest articles was not worth their time. In most cases, they hardly received any traffic from the post. Even if they received traffic, it didn't convert.

Some people have seen successful with guest posting and I won't say it's bad. It's an effective way to reach an audience, but blog commenting trumps guest posting.

Blog comments will go live almost instantly or within a few hours. There's no queue or waiting line. There's an enormous upside to blog commenting for people who value their time more than anything in the world.

I publish guest articles from time to time and I go absolutely crazy waiting for the date of publication. I know the article was approved and will be published after a month. It bothers me every passing day thinking about the day the article will go live. People who are solely dependent on guest posting go through 10 times more anxiety than I do.

Nobody likes waiting in a line. Nobody likes to wait for D-Day. We as human beings want everything instantly.

When I shop online, I always pay a little bit extra to receive the product within 24 hours. I can't wait. More than that, I value my time more than money. It's a chunk of my life. How can I gift wrap it and give it away?

Even if you ignore all the benefits of blog commenting, it's still my favorite, simply because it doesn't take months to get published, unlike a guest article.

**It's still a hidden advertising tool**

I will tell you why it's still hidden. Blog commenting is used as a tool for advertising by most online marketers, but there is a catch. Most online marketers are into SEO (search engine optimization). Blog commenting is a source to gain backlinks as well. So, instead of doing it for traffic, they do it for gaining backlinks.

The whole idea about blog commenting as a marketing tool is popular among online marketers, but the perception and the strategy is very different than what we are discussing in this book.

When the focus is to gain a backlink, the focus is on quantity rather than on quality. On top of everything, SEOr's focus on pages that have a high PR (page rank). They usually ignore the newly published fresh articles. The focus is mainly on old blog posts that have gained authority over time. When the main focus shifts from traffic to gaining backlink, the whole strategy shifts.

So, the fresh articles get fewer comments as compared to the old articles. This is a golden opportunity for new-age marketers like you and me. We have less competition when it comes to using blog commenting as an online marketing tool.

Whenever a blogger posts an article, he/she waits eagerly to see the first comment pop up. When it does, it makes them immensely happy and they immediately approve it from the admin panel. Thus, when you post a comment on a newly published fresh article, you have a bright 99.99% chance that your comment will be accepted within 24 hours.

## Build reputation management on Google.com for your name

I have talked about this earlier. Blog commenting can help you build your brand on Google itself. When you build a brand, the first thing a consumer does is to search for your brand name. If you are a solopreneur or an author, they will search for your name.

It's extremely important that the first page of Google is clean from any negative press. Not just the first page, your top 10 pages or 100 results on Google should have anything but positive press about your business. A single negative press can cost dearly my friend.

Google does a very good job of indexing all the comments just like they would for a normal guest post. Google loves fresh content. Hence, your comment posted on a fresh article is more likely to rank for your keyword term on Google.

So whenever someone searches for your name on Google, he will find all your websites, Twitter, Facebook, LinkedIn and YouTube profiles on the front page. Then, from the second page onward, it will be a heap of comments you have posted over the years. There will be no room for negative press to rank among all your indexed comments. Even if negative press does rank, it's more likely to be overshadowed by the huge positive press you will receive from these comments. After all, these comments will portray you as an authority figure.

**Each comment takes less than ten minutes**

I have a decent typing speed and it still takes me almost an hour to type 1000 words. If I were to write a guest post of 2000 words, it will take a minimum of two hours to write and an additional two hours for research, a total of four hours for the entire article. On top of that, I will have to hire a proofreader to polish my article before I send it over for publishing. It takes a hell of a lot of time to write and publish a well-researched article. This time is in addition to the weeks or even months you have to wait in order to get a guest article published on a blog.

Now, let's take a look at blog commenting. It takes approximately five minutes of speed-reading to read an article of 1000 words. Then it takes an additional five minutes to write and publish a comment. Can you see the time we can save?

Time is money and for business owners like us, it's more than money. It's a chunk of life. We have a limited amount of time and it's up to us how we want to invest our time. There are numerous books and courses on how to invest money, but hardly any books on how to invest time. Yeah, there are books that talk about saving time, but saving time is not equivalent to investing time. We need to invest time, not save it. Nobody has become rich by saving; they have become rich by investing.

Given a choice, how would you like to invest four hours of your time? Will you publish just one guest article or will you publish 20 comments?

Let's forget about the fact that a guest article will take months to get published, whereas a comment will be live online within 24 hours.

# Chapter 4

## How to Use Blog Commenting More Effectively?

Blog commenting is an art, just like writing an article. You can either write a plain blog comment or write an engaging blog comment that can result in conversion, sales and leads.

When you simply post a comment like anybody else, it mixes with the crowd. There's no special effect and hence it gets no special attention from the readers.

You comment need to be special. Your comment should be the only elephant in the room. You need visibility, remember?  Let's talk about a few surefire ways to use blog commenting more effectively.

**Use html <b>,<i> etc.**

You can post a plain comment or make it look more attractive by using bold or italic text. Of the comments I see, 99.99% are plain comments without any html formatting. Even I didn't bother to make the effort to use html tags, but after I wrote this book, I have promised myself to make the extra effort to use html tags with my commenting.

Html is not rocket science. When I ask you to add html tags, you don't have to use all coding language. Just remember two tags: <b> and <i>. <b> will make the text **bold** and <i> will make it *italics*. Here's an example of how to use them:

<b>This will make the sentence bold</b>
<i>This will make the sentence italics</i>

Most blog owners limit the usage of html in their comment fields. These two html tags are by far the most common tags that will work in almost every Wordpress blog you come across.

**Naming names**

While writing your article, try to call out names of other influencers. Most influencers will set up Google alerts for their name. When you write their names in the comment field, they will instantly receive an email notification from Google once the comment is indexed by Google.

This will help you build a connection with these influencers. If you are already active on their blogs, then it will add additional value to your relationship. The theory of reciprocation comes into play. When you call out their name, you are giving them visibility. You are helping them build their brand. You are helping them in their journey. They feel obliged to help you in return. It might come as a small help in the form of white-listing your IP on their blogs so that your comments go live instantly. They might also return the favor by mentioning your name somewhere or recommending your product or service to their audience.

Naming names has worked great for me. Who doesn't love being talked about? You tell me.

## Write a minimum of five to six paragraphs of comments - Approximately 300 words

When you write a blog comment, make sure you make it count. Write at least a five to six paragraph long comment. It will come out to approximately 300 words. Even if you post a 150 word comment, it's alright. Just try to stick to the 150+ word limit. It's really helpful in the long run.

If you want to be the elephant in the room, you need to have a big, fat comment.

When I read blogs as a reader, I hardly stop to

read comments that are less than 150 words. But when I see a comment that's 300 words long, I read it. I know that guy must have something valuable to add or else he wouldn't have taken the effort to write so much. A lot of people share the same perception as me.

You need to leverage this perception to make an impact. A big, fat comment will make an impact. It's impossible for our eyes to just ignore it.

**Use a real name every time**

There is no point in using a fake name to comment. The goal is to build your brand. If Coca-Cola starts blog commenting on sports and nutrition blogs as Pepsi, who will benefit?

It's silly, but a lot of people will post a comment using somebody else's name. They want to stay invisible. The only reason why they write a blog comment is to put forward their point.

Take the example of online reviewers. They gain nothing by leaving a review. Most of them will use a username. The only reason they leave a review is to be heard. They want the world to know what they think. In reality, the world doesn't give a crap about your opinion. People will only care about the value and the knowledge you offer.

Ever read an online review like this one?

*I hate this fucking restaurant. This is the shittiest place I have been to. The food is horrible. The manager is rude. The waiters are lazy. They should all die in an apocalypse.*

Reviews like the one above have absolutely no value for a reader. The reviewer doesn't want to educate or spread awareness about this restaurant. He just wants to take out his frustration and what better than an online review board?

Blog comments are somewhat similar. Tomorrow, you might come across a review of a particular product you have previously used, but had a bad experience with. Instead of taking out your frustration in a comment using a fake username, try to educate readers by offering more insight about this product. Have the guts to use a real name and speak honestly about what you liked and didn't like about this particular product. If you know of an alternate product that's better, link it out for others to easily find it.

When we really want to post a comment to help others, our whole behavior changes. We change from a self-absorbed person to a caring person. We need to change our mindset before starting out blog commenting as a strategy to build our brand.

It takes a great deal of patience to control our emotions. We learn and we grow.

**Either link to your blog or to your bio page, profile.**

There's a website field in the comment form where you can insert your website. It will drive traffic and readers will be able to learn a little more about you.

If you are posting it as an individual and not as a brand (using your real name), I recommend **not** linking to an e-commerce site. If you have a blog, link it to your blog. If you don't blog, link it to your bio page. If you don't even have a bio page, link it to your profile on a social network (Twitter, Facebook or LinkedIn).

You want people to click your website to find more about you. Remember, we do not use blog commenting to sell. We use it to build relationships. We need to be clear on our goals from the very beginning.

There are people who try to sell via their link on comments. I have even seen some people who will link to their E-Bay product page. What were they thinking? Will someone reading an article suddenly make up his/her mind to buy a product he is seeing for the first time? Readers are in the surfing mode. They are not in the buying mode. We need to understand that.

I link back to my Author website, www.Harsh.im which has all the details about me. I could have linked to one of my books, but will it do any good? Of course not. There's a reason why the hyperlink uses your "name" as an anchor text. People who click on your link will only do so if they want to know more about you. Before clicking your name, here's what they think, "Who is this guy?" Nobody thinks, "What is this guy selling?" Got the idea?

**Use special characters like tick, arrow, love, etc.**

I came across this idea while I was writing a description for my Kindle books on Amazon. Amazon has limited the usage of HTML in their book descriptions. I found out that special characters are still permitted and they can work together to make your content look more organized and professional.

I find all the text characters from http://text-symbols.com/.

**<u>Here's how you can use them:</u>**

It's raining outside ☂. It's getting cold ⛄. I am

going out to grab a cup of coffee ☐. I am listening to some music ♪. But, I have a flight to catch in an hour ✈. Bye . . . ✌ ツ

Instead of bullet points you can use ➤, ✦ , ➢ or ✔.

Instead of numbering, you can use ❶, ①, or Ⓐ.

You don't have to over use them like I just did here. It was just an example to show you how you can use different characters within your comment. Each comment can have just one special character. It will then look clean.

## Call out the writer by his/her first name

Whenever you are commenting on a blog, make sure to call out the writer by his/her first name. It personalizes the whole conversation. Instead of being a passerby, you become an audience.

What's the difference between an audience and a passerby?

A passerby is someone who will land on your blog from a website or a search engine, surf for a minute or two and will never return, whereas an audience constitutes your loyal fans and followers who eagerly wait for your next article.

A blogger survives on the mercy of his/her

audience. When you call someone out by their first name, you are no longer a passerby. You become a part of the audience who applauds good content. This builds a relationship between a blogger and his audience.

You take the first step of building this relationship by calling them out by their first name, just like a friend would call another friend.

Let me give you an example on how different it sounds when you call someone out by name.

**Instance 1:** Hello sir, can you excuse me?
**Instance 2:** Hello Mr., can you excuse me?
**Instance 3:** Hello John, can you excuse me?

Look at all the three sentences. Instance three personalizes the whole conversation because it uses the first name. Instance one and two, however, sounds like you are talking to a complete stranger. See the difference?

## Each reply to other blog commenters build connections

If you are just starting out in your commenting spree, you need to make as many friends as possible. Friends are "allies," remember? One way to do it is by building a connection with people who share a similar interest as you.

The best place to find these people are in the very same blogs where you will be commenting. Check out other blog commenters. If they have read the same article as you have, it means you both share similar interests or are from the same industry.

You can reply to their comments as well. Whenever I post a comment online, it's not just the blog owners who reply to me. There are other commenters who also reply, and I have built connections with these people. My comments start a conversation instead of just being "a comment."

Visit their blog and see if they have a blog. Start commenting on their blog as well.

**Don't advertise in the comment field**

Never try to advertise your product or your service in the comment field. It changes the whole purpose of blog commenting. Often, your comments will not be approved if you have a link in your comments. Blog owners usually remove the links in comments manually. I have seen it happen in many places.

If you have to link to a certain website for reference, then do not hyperlink it. Write it in this format: website.com as opposed to www.website.com.

The comment field is not for advertising. Treat it like a personal letter to the author.

**Use the same gravatar in all the websites**

You are building a brand for yourself. You expect people to know you by your "name" and "profile photo." Hence, it's really important to note that you **must** use a unique profile picture across all social networks. The same profile picture should also be used as your universal gravatar to post on all Wordpress blogs.

For people who are not familiar with the term gravatar, here's a quick answer:

A gravatar is a profile picture for Wordpress. Whenever you comment on any Wordpress blog, you need to provide your email ID in the comment field. Your email ID is linked to a particular profile picture. So, the next time you use that email in any Wordpress blog, the profile picture will show your photo. You can set up gravatar at http://gravatar.com/ . I highly recommend setting up your gravatar profile pic before starting your blog commenting journey. Most blog owners won't accept comments without a gravatar.

**Sign off using your name and salutation**

Add more personal feelings into your blog comment. Earlier, I have talked about calling out the blogger by his/her first name. It does a very good job as an introduction, but you need a damn good conclusion. In comments, a conclusion is referred to as the salutation and sign-off. It will leave an impression on the mind of the reader. It will imprint your name in their mind. After all, that's what you want, right? "To get the name out there."

You can use the following to conclude your comment:

Cheers!
XYZ

Signing off from <your city>
XYZ

Until next time . . .
XYZ

Or if you hold a particular position or if you are into a particular profession, you can add it below your name.

**Example:**

Cheers!
Harsh

Author, "Zero Advertising Cost, Blog Commenting Rocks"

The message should be subtle without any hidden agenda to promote your product or your service. The goal should be to educate readers about you and your work.

# Chapter 5

# My Personal Tips for You

In this chapter, I will offer a few personal tips that will help you in your blog commenting journey. You will find answers to where to find these blogs, how to use blog commenting to your advantage and how to drastically reduce your time commenting on blogs. There are many more tips. Let's get started!

**Stick to your niche**

It's extremely important that you stick to your niche. We as human beings have very limited time for ourselves. There are millions of others out there who compete with us for the same audience and exposure. We need to be on top of our game in order to win this.

One of the biggest mistakes people make is by focusing on a lot of things all at once. When it comes to blog commenting, you might be both an app developer and a fitness trainer. If you focus on two niches all at once, your efficiency decreases. We fall under into the category of "Jack of all trades, master of none."

In order to dominate a particular niche, we should focus on just once niche. Ask yourself, do you want to first dominate the app industry or the fitness industry? Once you have your answer, choose one and stick to it. I am not asking you to stick to a particular niche for months at a stretch. If you are just starting out, stick to it for at least three months to start with. Once you are fairly established as a reputable blog commenter in your industry, you can move on to the next niche. Late, you can alternate posting on a niche every 15 days.

While doing so, you might come across a lot of other blogs. Say for example you are on a website about app development. You might come across a website banner that links to a Wordpress theme website. Don't waste your time lurking around in those blogs. It's of no use to your business. It's like being on Facebook while you should be at work. Our "monkey brain" enjoys such distractions. Don't let it. Control it.

**Focus on high traffic blogs (be where the audience is)**

We struggle with time. We all do. As I am writing this book today, I woke up at 4:30 a.m. this morning because I have a deadline to write 15,000 words within two days. I am sure you have similar deadlines in your business all the time.

It's our responsibility to use our time in the best possible way. Even when it comes to blog commenting, one can waste a lot of time posting on blogs with little or no traffic at all. What's the use?

Focus on on high-traffic blogs only, blogs that are worth your time. If you don't, you will end up posting hundreds of comments without any result.

Be where the audience is. Would it be helpful for you to open a physical shop in a location where there is absolutely no traffic? Or, will you open your shop in a location that's the most happening place in the city?

Keep looking for blogs with traffic. That's where you want to be. There are a lot of ways to find out whether or not a blog has traffic. You can install the Alexa toolbar. Alexa.com is an analytical website that provides a global ranking based on a site's traffic. A global rank within 100,000 is considered to be a good choice to start with. Another way to know the traffic of a site is by installing the Semrush plugin. Semrush.com is again an analytical company that tracks search engine keywords from which a website receives traffic (both paid and organic).

Semrush offers a quote for each website, which is called the "Semrush SE traffic price." It estimates the money one must spend every month to receive the same amount of traffic to his blog. So, if the "Semrush SE traffic price" is $500.00, it means that you would have to spend $500.00 to receive the same online exposure. It indicates what a website is worth.

Personally, I prefer to comment on blogs with a minimum Semrush price of $300.00 or more.

### Search Google for your keywords. Check out the first two pages if they are blogs

It takes ages for a small business to rank on the first page of Google for their favorite keywords. It has become even more difficult now-a-days, since Google has rolled out multiple updates to combat Blackhat SEO.

The first page is now mainly dominated by big brands. Small business owners are left to target long-tail keywords for traffic. Now, imagine if you had the opportunity to write a guest post on a website that's already sitting on the first page of Google for your keyword. You would obviously take it because you know it will offer you massive exposure for your brand.

How about blog comments then? Yes, now that we have our own little secret weapon, it's time to use it against some big guns.

Search for your respective keyword on Google. Check to see if there are any blogs on the first two pages. If there are, put them on your list (I prefer to use an excel file) to regularly read and post comments.

Even though your website is not on the first page of Google, you can advertise your business for free on websites that are already on the first page of Google. How wonderful is that?

Don't get me wrong, by "advertise" I mean "branding." not 'classified ads or "link dropping." I have to clarify this because I have received emails and reviews from people who often misinterpret my statements.

## Use BuzzSumo to find articles on any given topic with max social shares

BuzzSumo is one of my favorite tools to find new blogs. It has a lot of incredible features. Whenever you search for a particular keyword, it will list a number of websites based on the amount of social shares it has received. It helps to find an article that went viral previously.

You can also filter the search result based on interviews, guest posts, infographics, giveaways, video posts and general articles.

You can also find people who have Tweeted a particular website.

I will tell you how it will be useful. Let's say I am a retailer who sells a weight loss product called "Herbal Slim."

I will search for "acai berry," "African mango," "green coffee," etc. on BuzzSumo. These are all weight loss products. I will find the list of articles that has received the highest number of social shares and then start commenting on them.

I can also find the people who have Tweeted these articles. I can start following them on Twitter or replying to their tweets. They will start following me and we can build even more connections from there.

The possibilities are endless. The secret is to keep doing what seem to be working at the moment.

**Create a separate email ID:**

I highly recommend that you create a brand new email ID for the purpose of blog commenting. You don't want to receive bulk emails on your primary email address every time someone replies to one of your comments. Creating a new email ID only takes a minute. Please do it.

You should then go to gravatar.com and update this new email address there. This new email ID will be linked to your gravatar photo.

Once you are done, find the blogs you can comment on. Start with 50 to 60 blogs. Subscribe to their mailing list or newsletter so that you will receive a notification whenever a new article is published.

You need to pick these blogs based on traffic and authority. There's no point in wasting your time on small blogs.

**If you know an influencer, find his blog.**

I have previously asked you to find blogs and then interact with the audience as well, but there are times when you might have a different need, the need to connect with an influencer. You will surely follow him or her on twitter, Facebook and every other social networking site, but that's not enough.

Try to determine if he has a blog. If he does, start commenting on his blog. Focus on only interacting with him. This time you aren't trying to impress his audience but him.

Get in the limelight. A relationship with an

influencer goes a long way. He will eventually introduce you to his tribe. You will get to know other influencers. It will eventually build your authority and by hanging around with lions, even you will become a lion.

**Do you plan to publish a guest article somewhere? Become a ninja blog commenter first.**

There are thousands of websites that accepts guest posts. They receive hundreds of entries every week. They can only accept one or two. Apart from offering them the right pitch, there are other qualities. They will see and research your background. If you have already built a personal relationship with them, your chances of getting approved increase by 1000%.

All of the psychological factors will start affecting their judgment while going through the list of all the pitches.

If you are an active commenter in the community, the theory of reciprocation will come into play. They will feel like giving you the opportunity to publish your guest article for all the love and support you have shown them.

The concept of "likelihood" is obviously a big factor. They already like you. They are going to be biased in their judgment.

The concept of "belonging" is another factor that will affect their judgment. They will see you as one of their own. When you post regularly, in particular on blog or in a community, you are a part of the community. It's like favoring a family member over a complete stranger. Got the idea?

There might be other psychological factors of which I am not. I am not a psychologist. These three are the ones I can come up with. Even these three are very powerful to increase your chances of getting your pitch for a guest article accepted.

You can use the hidden weapon of blog commenting to stay ahead of the game. You can in fact dominate your competitors because you have an unfair advantage, "this book."

**Find the biggest blogs in our industry**

Previously, I have asked you to subscribe to a list of around 50 to 60 blogs to begin with. You might not have the time and energy to focus on all the blogs, so find the blogs with the most amount of traffic. Make it a habit of commenting on each and every article they publish.

It's important that you focus on high-traffic blogs more than the rest. These blogs will offer you the biggest opportunities.

Big blog = High Traffic = Better reach = More audience = More Opportunities

## Use "Dragon Naturally Speaking" to reduce the time it takes to comment.

Typing can take a lot of time. I can understand that. Fortunately, there are some alternatives. There is a lot of text-to-speech software available. The most common one is perhaps the built-in feature on our smartphones and tablets.

For computers, the best and the most accurate text-to-speech software is "Dragon Naturally Speaking." It can reduce your time by more than half. If it takes you ten minutes to write something, it will take you hardly a minute or two to read it out. Imagine the amount of time you can save.

I still prefer typing as opposed to talking. Moreover, I need to practice typing to increase my speed. I am a writer so the situation is different for me. If you are a business owner, you might want to try out "[Dragon naturally speaking](#)." You can find it on Amazon.

There are some free alternatives like the built-in text-to-voice feature on the iPad. It's not as accurate as the former, but it does the job.

In the next chapter, we will talk about a few do's and don'ts. We have almost hit the end of this book. I hope that it has been an enjoyable read so far. Alright, let's move on to the next chapter.

# Chapter 6

## Do's and Don'ts

There are standard rules in every game, in every business, in every platform. Even in blog commenting, we have some rules. It's always better to play by the book.

**Never advertise**

Blog commenting is never for the purpose of advertising. On average a blog owner receives about 50 junk comments posted by individuals to advertise their product and services. On top of that, a blog owner also receives hundreds of spam comments posted by automated bots. It's frustrating for a blogger.

Even the slightest smell of advertising can act against you. The acceptance chances will go down from 99.99% to less than 50% with just a single link to your product or services.

Blog commenting is not for people who want instant gratification. We are marketers and we need to plan long term. I have already talked about many advantages of blog commenting and how they can help you in your overall marketing strategy.

Think long-term rather than short-term.

**Never use abusive language**

It's unavoidable that you will meet a couple of idiots along the way. There's no point in wasting your time taking on a war with someone on the internet. Just mind your own business and move on. Everybody will have his/her opinion. You can't control them. What you can control is yourself.

Do not use abusive or hateful language. You don't want to portray yourself as a hater in an online community. Remember, you are branding yourself or your business.

Being abusive can only be harmful for your brand. Period.

**Never use a keyword instead of a real name**

How many times have you come across a comment that has been posted using a "keyword?" If yes, say "aye."

How silly is that? People who expect that posting a blog comment using a keyword will help them in SEO are delusional. I practiced SEO for the last seven years, until I retired last year. Out of all the SEO strategies, I can tell you one thing for sure. Using a keyword instead of your real name will not help you rank on Google. This is a big myth. Google has evolved, they have updated their algorithm. Now, they are in fact punishing sites by devaluing them from search results if they use a keyword in blog comments.

If you are posting it as a brand, you can use your "brand name" instead of your "real name," but never use a keyword to post a comment. It not only looks unprofessional, but de-personalized and stupid.

**Writing a one-liner is a waste of time.**

Writing a one-liner is a complete waste of time. You will never get recognized. I am sure you read a couple of blogs weekly. As a reader, do you every read those one-liner comments?

However, a big, fat comment of 300 words will instantly catch our eyes. We don't see such comments very often, so the few we do see grabs our eyeballs.

"Be the elephant in the room because everyone can spot an elephant."

It is better to write one 300 word comment than

ten 30 word comments. We need to be consistent if we want to get noticed. It takes two to three months of continuous hard work before you will see any results, so don't lose heart if it takes a while. Opportunities will start showing up automatically.

**It means you will need to post daily**

Persistence is the key. Don't plan out a schedule where you set aside only the weekends to do blog commenting. It won't work. You need to comment daily and religiously. Think of it like any other task, like checking and replying to emails. Do you check and reply to emails daily? How do you find time to type so much? And if you can type an email, why can't you type a comment?

These are all the questions I ask myself whenever I procrastinate. Once we start seeing new opportunities opening up in front of us, we will start to take commenting lightly and focus on other stuff.

It backfires. Success becomes a temporary state and soon fades away. Do not stop even when the opportunities start pouring in. Exploit it unless and until you are capable of spending thousands on advertising costs. Once you have unlimited money to spend money on advertising, you can shift your goals from time-intensive tasks like blog commenting to running viral campaigns that takes a fraction of your time to reach a huge audience.

After all, our life is a reflection of how we spend our time. Make smart investments when it is time. Focus on blog commenting during the time you don't have enough of an advertising budget. Once you have the money to spend on advertising, I don't see the need to post manually on blogs. Will Bill Gates post on webmaster blogs? Of course not. His time is much more valuable than that.

After a certain point in time, you can hire a couple of VA's to do the job for you. Once you become a brand from person, you can hire almost anybody to outsource the job. The next time you see a comment posted by someone who signs as "Business advisor to Bill Gates," it is certainly going to raise eyeballs. We can do the same, but before that we need to build a brand for ourselves, a brand that everyone can relate to. Blog commenting gives us access to a completely free advertising channel. Let's exploit it when the time is right.

# A Note to My Readers

# Review If You Want, I Won't Force You

Nothing makes me happier than to see my reader's reviews. I go through every one of them.

Every day, they motivate me to write better. I am still a child at heart. Every time I read a review, my eyes glow. I read each review at least five to six times because it makes me realize that I am doing something good to help people.

Each and every review counts. I know I can count on you because you have also struggled to get reviews for your books. You know the importance of reviews more than anyone else.

You don't owe me anything but if you want others to find this book, your review is really important. After you have paid me and brought this book, you have absolutely no obligation to return a review. You have paid money and I offered you this book. I understand that this was a pure business transaction.

But, I am asking you as a friend to do me a favor. A favor is all I ask. If life gives me a chance to return that favor to you, I surely will. That's a promise.

**Here's the direct link to leave a review:**

Regards,

*Harshajyoti Das*

# Contact Info:

- **Fan Email:** author@harsh.im
- **Interview/guestposting/Press requests:** press@harsh.im
- **Amazon Author Profile:** http://www.amazon.com/author/harshajyotidas
- **Twitter:** http://twitter.com/jr_sci
- **Facebook:** https://www.facebook.com/harshajyotidas.author
- **LinkedIn:** http://in.linkedin.com/pub/harshajyoti-das/17/28b/52
- **Google+:** https://plus.google.com/+HarshajyotiDas

**Author Website:** Harsh.Im

**CEO at Munmi IT Solutions LLP:** Munmi.org

**Founder of:** FireYourMentor.com

**MAILING LIST:** http://www.fireyourmentor.com/70-secrets-revealed/

2014 by *Harshajyoti Das*

All rights reserved.

**All Rights Reserved. No part of this publication may be reproduced in any form or by any means, including scanning, photocopying, or otherwise without prior written permission of the copyright holder.**

Disclaimer and Terms of Use: The Author and Publisher has strived to be as accurate and complete as possible in the creation of this book, notwithstanding the fact that he does not warrant or represent at any time that the contents within are accurate due to the rapidly changing nature of the Internet. While all attempts have been made to verify information provided in this publication, the Author and Publisher assumes no responsibility for errors, omissions, or contrary interpretation of the subject matter herein. Any perceived slights of specific persons, peoples, or organizations are unintentional. In practical advice books, like anything else in life, there are no guarantees of results. Readers are cautioned to rely on their own judgment about their individual circumstances and act accordingly. This book is not intended for use as a source of legal, medical, business, accounting or financial advice. All readers are advised to seek services of competent professionals in the legal, medical, business, accounting, and finance fields.

First Published, 2014

www.ingramcontent.com/pod-product-compliance
Lightning Source LLC
Chambersburg PA
CBHW071801170526
45167CB00003B/1128